THE VALUE OF FORESIGHT

The Story of Thomas Jefferson

VALUE COMMUNICATIONS, INC.
PUBLISHERS
LA JOLLA, CALIFORNIA

THE VALUE OF FORESIGHT

The Story of
Thomas Jefferson

BY ANN DONEGAN JOHNSON

The Value of Foresight is part of the ValueTales series.

The Value of Foresight text copyright © 1979 by Ann Donegan
Johnson. Illustrations copyright © 1979 by Value
Communications, Inc.
All rights reserved under International and Pan American
Copyright Conventions.
No part of this book may be reproduced in any manner
whatsoever without written permission from the publisher,
except in the case of brief quotations embodied in reviews
and articles.

First Edition
Manufactured in the United States of America
For information write to: ValueTales, P.O. Box 1012
La Jolla, CA 92038

Library of Congress Cataloging in Publication Data

Johnson, Ann Donegan.
    The value of foresight.

    (ValueTales)
    SUMMARY: A biography of Thomas Jefferson
emphasizing his lasting contributions to his country.
    1. Jefferson, Thomas, Pres. U.S., 1743-1826—Juvenile
literature. 2. Presidents—United States—Biography—
Juvenile literature. 3. Prudence—Juvenile literature.
[1. Jefferson, Thomas, Pres. U.S., 1743-1826.
2. Presidents. 3. Prudence] I. Title.
E332.79.J64   973.4'6'0924 [B] [92]   79-19548

ISBN 0-916392-42-2

Dedicated to Mary, Marsha, Nancy, Doris, Patsy, Judy, Dolly and Diane

This tale is about Thomas Jefferson, who used foresight to help determine the future of America. More historical facts about Thomas Jefferson can be found on page 63.

Once upon a time...

in the long-ago days when our country was still a British colony, there lived a tall, sandy-haired young man named Thomas Jefferson.

Thomas lived with his mother and his sisters at Shadwell, a plantation in the part of Virginia we now call Albemarle County. He rode horses and he hunted. He fished and he swam in the Rivanna River. And he studied Latin and Greek.

Thomas Jefferson's father died when the boy was fourteen, so young Tom learned early to think for himself. By the time he was seventeen, he had decided that Latin and Greek were very good, but that there were other things he needed to know.

"I want to go to Williamsburg to study at the College of William and Mary," he said to his guardian. "I want to learn mathematics."

8

Tom's guardian was delighted with what he heard. "You are showing foresight, Tom. Planning ahead for the future is important!" He gave his permission, and Tom set out for Williamsburg.

Williamsburg was a terribly exciting place for the lad from Shadwell. The college there was the second oldest college in the colonies. The town was also the capital of Virginia, and the governor lived there in an elegant mansion called the Governor's Palace.

The governor was not elected by the people. Because Virginia was a British colony, he was appointed by the king of England.

9

At William and Mary, there were many fine professors. One of them, a man named William Small, taught mathematics and physics, astronomy and philosophy. He was a Scot who loved to teach, and he enjoyed students who loved to learn. He and Tom got along famously.

"Come, Tom," he said to Jefferson one day. "I'd like you to meet some friends of mine." Small introduced Tom to Francis Fauquier, who was the royal governor of Virginia, and to George Wythe. "I've heard of George Wythe," Jefferson whispered to Small. "He's one of the most brilliant lawyers in the colonies, isn't he?"

"Indeed he is," said Small. "He's a great Latin and Greek scholar, too. Pay attention to him, Tom. You can learn a great deal from a man like Wythe."

Governor Fauquier loved to entertain, and Tom was often invited to the palace. Fauquier liked music, too, and Tom could play the violin. So Tom became a part of the governor's chamber music group.

When he wasn't playing, Tom listened to the conversations in the governor's drawing room. He heard George Wythe and the other distinguished guests argue about law and justice. They talked about duty and philosophy, and even about science. Tom was fascinated. He paid such close attention, and he asked such keen questions, that the other guests were intrigued by this lad from the country.

"The boy is well read and he's got an excellent mind," said William Small. "He's a young man who's going places."

13

Jefferson did go places in Williamsburg. He went to the Governor's Palace, of course. He also went to dances and to hunts. He had tea with some of the leading people in the town, but before the end of the year, he found he was not happy.

"I'm wasting time!" he said to himself one morning. "I'm wasting more time than if I'd stayed home at Shadwell."

"I'm glad you've finally realized it," said a small, chiming sort of voice.

Tom blinked. He thought he was hearing things—and seeing things, too. His pocket watch, which had been lying quietly on the bureau, was now looking cross and scolding him rather severely.

"Not that there's anything really wrong with dancing and hunting," said the watch. "However, if you're going to spend all of your time at college dancing and being agreeable to people, you might as well send *me* back to Shadwell, for I'm certainly doing you no good!"

Tom chuckled. He knew very well that pocket watches do not talk. He was only listening to his own good sense. But what he heard pleased him.

"All right," he said. "From now on, I'll really study!"

15

Tom did study hard all that summer. He went back to college in the fall and worked even harder. Sometimes he got out of bed and began his studies before the sun was up.

He kept his watch with him, perhaps because he liked to discuss things out loud, or perhaps because he thought it was fun to have an imaginary friend. He named the watch Chimes, as if it were a big, important clock. He paid attention to Chimes, and he didn't waste time.

At twilight, after Tom had been studying hard all day, Chimes would remind him that it was time to take a break. Off they'd go to run for a mile or two.

16

When Tom was nineteen, he graduated from William and Mary. He knew Latin, Greek, French, and Italian. He had read the writings of the ancient philosophers, and he had studied the works of the eighteenth-century scientists. In an age when books were expensive and rather scarce, he had a library of hundreds of volumes.

"I'm proud of you," said Chimes. "Do you know that you're one of the most educated men in Virginia?"

Tom grinnned. "It's wonderful how much may be done if we're always doing," he said.

Now Tom had to decide how he would spend the rest of his life. "It might be pleasant simply to be a Virginia planter," he said. "But this is a new land, and I'd like to help make it a good one. I want to be a lawyer."

"That's showing some foresight!" applauded Chimes. "We're going to need lawyers in the American colonies."

In those days there were no law schools. Young men who wanted to be lawyers learned about the law by reading, by watching, and by doing. They read law books. They ran errands for lawyers and helped them prepare briefs. They also watched the more experienced lawyers who appeared in court.

18

Tom went to work for his friend, George Wythe. When he learned something new, he wrote it down in his notebook. Tom found that he loved the law. "I've made the right choice, Chimes," he said to his ticking little watch.

"I thought you would," said Chimes, "and I'm glad to see that you have the foresight to take notes on everything you learn."

Tom was twenty-three when he passed his examinations and became a lawyer. Although he was young, he was very successful. Many prominent people wanted him to defend them in court.

But Tom soon found that lawsuits could be tiresome. "Chimes, I think I could do more for myself and for my fellowman if I went into politics," he said.

"Excellent!" cried Chimes. "You'd have a hand in making the law, instead of just practicing it in a courtroom."

And so, in 1769, when Tom Jefferson was twenty-six years old, he was elected a member of the House of Burgesses. This was a group of representatives chosen by the people to help govern Virginia.

The meetings of the representatives were held in Williamsburg, so Tom was back among his old friends of college days, which pleased him very much.

But while Tom was busy with politics, a terrible thing happened at Shadwell. The house caught fire and burned to the ground!

"Your wonderful library!" moaned Chimes. He and Tom stood looking at the blackened ruins. "All the books you gathered while you were in college. All your law books. They meant so much to you, and now they're gone!"

Tom sighed. "The only thing that was saved was my violin," he said. "Never mind. It can't be helped. I'll start a new library, for I must have books."

Then Chimes had a marvelous idea. Do you know what it was?

"You can start a new house, too," he told Tom. "You're interested in architecture. You'll enjoy working on a house of your very own."

Tom began to smile. "That would be fun," he agreed.

"See that hill on the other side of the Rivanna?" asked Chimes. "Remember how you used to cross the river so you could climb that hill? You used to sit on the top and study. You called the hill Monticello because that means 'little hill' in Italian. And you said you'd like to build a house there when you grew up."

"I remember!" exclaimed Tom. "Of course, I remember. And I *will* build a house. I will build a beautiful house, and I will fill it with marvelous things!"

So Tom and Chimes moved into a tiny brick cottage on Monticello, and Tom started working on the plans for his wonderful house on the hill.

While Tom was still in the House of Burgesses and Monticello was
still being built, something happened that changed Tom's whole
life. It all began at a party, when a most charming young lady
named Martha Wayles sat down at a harpsichord and began to
play. She sang, too, and very sweetly.

"She's lovely!" said Tom to Chimes. "Chimes, don't you think
she's lovely?"

Chimes laughed a tinkling laugh. "I don't believe it matters a bit
what I think," he said to Tom. "Unless I'm mistaken, you've just
fallen in love!"

Chimes was absolutely right. In the days that followed, Tom called often at the Forest, the plantation where the young lady lived with her father. Tom played the violin with Martha Wayles. He danced with Martha. He went riding with Martha.

Then, on New Year's Day in 1772, what do you suppose happened?

Tom and Martha were married.

Tom returned to Monticello with his bride.

"I'm sorry the house is not finished, Martha," apologized Tom.

"That's all right. We shall work on it together," replied Martha, reassuringly.

"I have so many plans for it!" said Tom, excitedly.

Martha smiled to herself. "Is there anything this man isn't interested in?" she thought.

Tom and Martha tended to all the details that would make Monticello a treasure. Tom planned the flower gardens and laid out the orchards. He kept careful records of their growth in his garden book.

"You know, Chimes," he said, "science is my passion, and law, my duty."

29

But while Tom was busy building and planting, the laws of the thirteen colonies were being challenged by the people. These laws were made in the English Parliament in London by men who had never set foot in America. And too often these laws had to do with taxes. The people felt that they were being taxed unfairly.

"Taxation without representation is tyranny!" cried the Americans.

The men in Parliament paid no attention. Instead, they put a tax on tea. Then they said that only one company, the East India Company, could bring tea into the colonies. The people in America were very angry!

In Boston there was a group of patriots called the Sons of Liberty. When the tea ships from the East India Company sailed into Boston Harbor in December 1773, they sent word to the governor. The tea ships must be sent back to England. The governor refused. The Sons of Liberty disguised themselves as Mohawk Indians and stormed down to the harbor. They climbed aboard the ships and threw more than three hundred huge chests of tea into the ocean. This was called the Boston Tea Party.

Now the British were angry. On June 1, 1774, they tried to punish the colonists by closing the port of Boston.

"That's dreadful!" exclaimed Tom to Chimes. "The worst of it is, the people here in Virginia may not realize that trouble for one colony means trouble for all."

"But they must realize it!" said Chimes. "Isn't there something you can do?"

Tom nodded. "Perhaps there is," he said. Then he got the House of Burgesses to proclaim June 1 a day of fasting and prayer to protest the closing of the port.

Jefferson wrote a paper about the rights of British Americans. In it Tom said that the English Parliament had no authority in the colonies. He also said that the colonists' allegiance to the king of England should be of their own free will and not forced.

"They won't like that in London," said Chimes. "In fact, even some Americans won't like it."

Chimes was right. No one in London liked Tom's ideas. And many colonists felt Tom had been too critical. Just the same, Jefferson was becoming known as a writer on matters having to do with the rights of the colonists.

The patriots in America had formed committees to exchange information and ideas. In 1774, members from these committees called for a congress of the colonies. Twelve of the thirteen colonies sent representatives to Philadelphia, Pennsylvania, for this Continental Congress. They felt that, if they got together and spoke as a united people, they could persuade the British government to recognize their rights.

The First Continental Congress was not successful. War between the patriots and the British broke out in April 1775.

By now Thomas Jefferson had written many marvelous papers on why America should be free of British rule. Tom set out for Philadelphia to be part of the Second Continental Congress.

"This is an honor, Chimes," said Tom. "I'll be working with people like John Adams and Benjamin Franklin! And this congress won't be like the first one. This congress will really get things done!"

After he arrived in Philadelphia, Tom Jefferson learned what was really in store for him.

A committee had been appointed to draw up a statement declaring to the world that America was a free and independent country. Tom was to be a member of the committee. And because he was so well known for the papers he had written, he was asked to put the ideas of the group into writing.

Tom was a brave young man, but the idea of composing such a declaration frightened him. "I'm so young," he said. He looked at John Adams, the representative from Massachusetts. "Why don't you write the declaration?" he suggested.

Adams shook his head. "You write ten times better than I do," he told Tom.

"Oh, Chimes," sighed Tom when he was alone. The pens were ready, and the crisp, blank paper was in front of him on his portable writing desk. "This is the most important thing I've ever done. It may be the most important thing I'll ever do!"

"Then, as you write, look ahead the way you usually do," said Chimes. "Think of how this country can become a great nation once it is free."

Tom nodded. "I will have to write in terms that are very plain and very firm."

To be both plain and firm takes care. After seventeen days, Tom returned to the congress with his declaration. It was not a long document, but it contained statements that made the hearts of the patriots beat faster.

Jefferson had written that "all men are created equal" and that people have certain rights, including the right to "life, liberty, and the pursuit of happiness!"

The delegates to the congress made one or two changes in Jefferson's declaration. Then the great men who had come to Philadelphia to found a new nation began to sign the Declaration of Independence, pledging their lives, their fortunes, and their honor to uphold it.

There were celebrations when the signing was over. The church bells rang out in the city. There were parades, too. People cheered for the American soldiers as they marched by in their uniforms.

It was July 4, 1776—our nation's birthday.

The bell-ringing and the parades did not last long. The British refused to recognize America's independence. The fighting continued. In fact, it continued for five more years. Finally, the British realized they could not win, and in 1781 the British General Cornwallis surrendered to American forces at Yorktown.

During part of the war, Tom Jefferson was governor of Virginia. It was Tom who ordered out the militia when his state was invaded by British troops. And one day, when Tom was quietly attending to his duties at Monticello, a young officer rushed in.

"Mr. Jefferson, the British are in Charlottesville now," said the young man. "There's a party of them on the way here to arrest you!"

Jefferson thanked the young man politely. He had already sent Martha and the children to stay with neighbors. As he left the house, he could see the soldiers and their horses in the distance.

Protected by the shadows of the trees, Jefferson ran to the stables. "I'd better leave quickly," he thought.

"It's the only thing to do," Chimes said. "It doesn't take much foresight to know that the British would love to capture the governor of Virginia—and the author of the Declaration of Independence."

The British were disappointed when they galloped up to Monticello and found no sign of Jefferson. But they damaged nothing. When Jefferson returned to his home after the British had gone, he found it almost as he had left it.

Jefferson was happy that his beloved Monticello was unharmed, for the house had become like a living thing to him. He devoted so much time and energy to planning and building it, and to inventing unique devices for it, such as a swivel chair and a clock with cannon ball weights. The house became more and more interesting and more and more beautiful.

But not long after Tom Jefferson returned to Monticello, a terrible tragedy overtook him.

His beloved Martha died.

At first it seemed that Jefferson would never be happy again. He walked up and down in the library at Monticello—up and down, up and down—day and night.

"Tom, you can't go on like this," whispered Chimes. "You have to go out into the sunlight and live the rest of your life."

But still Tom Jefferson paced and grieved.

"What about your children?" cautioned Chimes. Now Jefferson began to pay attention, for he knew that the voice of Chimes was the voice of his own conscience.

"You've always been a sensible man with lots of foresight," said Chimes. "What will become of your children if you bury yourself in grief? And what about your country? The war is over now, but the real work of building a new nation is still to be done. Don't you want to be a part of it?"

What do you suppose Tom Jefferson did when he thought about these things?

He tried hard to overcome his grief. It was very difficult. Many months passed, but the day finally came when he went back into politics.

Generally Tom began to feel happier. Things were better for him. And he felt real pride in 1786 when the Virginia House of Delegates passed his Bill for Establishing Religious Freedom. "Perhaps, at last, we're beginning to realize that you can't force a man to think a certain way," he said.

In 1789, George Washington appointed Jefferson to be his secretary of state, and in 1796 Tom became vice-president under John Adams. Then, in 1800, the people elected Thomas Jefferson the third president of the United States.

"It's a huge responsibility," thought Jefferson as he moved into the White House.

But then it seemed that Jefferson could hear the tiny, chiming voice of his little friend. "You can do it," said the voice. "Do it the way you do everything—with good sense and great care."

Of course, Jefferson lived surrounded by the results of his own foresight. He had helped to plan the city of Washington, and he was the first president to be inaugurated there.

But the new president's concerns extended far beyond Washington. There was the matter of New Orleans, for instance. It was an important seaport, vital to American shipping, but the French owned it.

"It doesn't seem right for another country to own this great port," said Jefferson. "It isn't wise, and it could threaten our security."

After Congress said $2 million could be spent, Jefferson wrote to
Robert Livingston, his minister in France, instructing him to try to
purchase New Orleans and West Florida from Napoleon, the ruler
of France. Then Jefferson sent James Monroe to help with the
negotiations.

Livingston and Monroe found that Napoleon was willing enough to sell New Orleans. In fact, Napoleon wanted to sell the entire Louisiana Territory. "What will the United States give for the land?" asked Talleyrand, Napoleon's minister.

The question took the Americans' breath away. The Louisiana Territory was a vast area—more than 827,000 square miles. It was bounded on the north by Canada, and it extended west to parts of Colorado, Wyoming, and Montana.

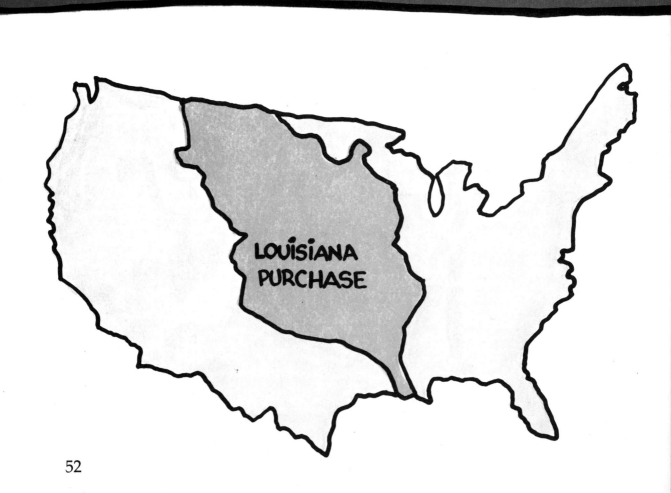

"We're a new country," thought Jefferson, when he heard of Talleyrand's offer. "We will keep growing. We'll need more room before we're through." And in 1803 he bought the entire territory for $15 million, or about three cents per acre!

"Now you're really showing foresight!" cried Chimes. He had not been so excited since the signing of the Declaration of Independence back in Philadelphia.

No sooner had he acquired the Louisiana Territory than Jefferson sent for Captain Meriwether Lewis. Lewis was an old friend of the president's, and Jefferson knew he was a skilled leader and explorer.

"I believe it's high time that we knew more about our country," said Jefferson to Lewis. "We have hundreds and thousands of acres that we've never even seen. Some people say it would be easy to get to the Pacific Ocean by following the Missouri River. What do you think?"

Lewis grinned, for he had a good idea what President Jefferson had in mind. "I think we should go and find out," he said.

"And I think congress would vote the money for an expedition," said Jefferson happily. His scientific curiosity was aroused, and he was excited at the idea of the adventure west, and of the information Lewis might bring back to him.

Lewis asked William Clark to go with him as second in command. In May 1804, the two explorers left St. Louis, Missouri, together with a band of forty well-trained men. They traveled up the Missouri River to North Dakota, and then spent the winter of 1805 in Indian villages there.

When spring came, the men went on by water as far as they could. Then they crossed the Rockies and the Bitterroot Mountains. At last they reached the lands where the rivers flowed west, toward the Pacific Ocean.

Their trip took more than two years and taught them, among other things, that traveling by land across the American continent was *not* easy.

"What an adventure!" cried Tom Jefferson when he read the notes and the diaries of the explorers. "And it's been a valuable adventure. Now we know about the land between here and the Pacific—the mountains, the plant life, the soil, the minerals—and especially the lives of the Indians."

"Foresight can really pay off, can't it?" said Chimes.

Thomas Jefferson was sixty-six years old when he retired from the presidency and went home again to his beloved Monticello. He was as full of plans and ideas as ever.

"What are we going to do now?" asked Chimes.

"We're going to build a school," Jefferson announced. "I want to design the buildings, supervise the construction, choose the teachers. I want to plan the whole thing myself!"

Jefferson plunged into work on the project with all the enthusiasm in his nature.

He was a skilled architect now, so he drew up plans for the buildings. He was a surveyor, so he measured the sites. He had worked with bricklayers and carpenters before, and he did it again. He sent to Europe for the best scholars of the day to come and teach the young people of Virginia.

"I have a feeling that what you're doing will last," said Chimes, "and that this school will become a great university."

"I should hope so," said Thomas Jefferson. "What I'm doing today isn't only for today, any more than the Louisiana Purchase was for its day, or the Declaration of Independence was for 1776. What I'm doing is for us, and for those who'll come after us."

Jefferson was eighty-two when the University of Virginia opened its doors in 1825. The country he had helped to found was nearly fifty years old. Jefferson was a happy man.

Thomas Jefferson lived in a time when this nation was being founded, and he played an important part in planning and building for its future.

We now live in the time he planned and built for.

It takes foresight to build for the future, but wouldn't it be exciting to create something that would last two hundred years—or more!

The End

Historical Facts ·

Thomas Jefferson was born on April 13 (April 2, Old Style) at Shadwell, a tobacco plantation in Virginia owned by his father, Peter Jefferson. Thomas's mother, Jane Randolph Jefferson, was a member of one of Virginia's more distinguished families.

Peter Jefferson died when Thomas was fourteen. He left his son valuable land and insisted that he be given a complete education. In 1760, Jefferson entered the College of William and Mary in Williamsburg, the colonial capital of Virginia. He graduated in 1762 and then studied law for five years under George Wythe, one of the finest legal minds in Virginia.

Although Jefferson became a successful lawyer, he never really enjoyed practicing law. After seven years, he gave up that profession to go into politics. He became a member of the Virginia House of Burgesses in 1769. His first act in the House was an unsuccessful attempt to pass a bill allowing people to free their slaves.

In 1772, Jefferson married Martha Wayles Skelton, a widow. With her, he lived at Monticello, the beautiful home he designed and built. They had six children, one son and five daughters.

It was at this time that many of the colonists were growing tired of British control and policies under King George III. The colonists particularly objected to the taxes imposed upon them by Parliament in the Sugar Act (1764), the Stamp Act (1765), and the Townshend Acts (1767). Jefferson began writing essays against British domination. These essays were widely circulated and earned him a reputation as a fine writer.

When Thomas Jefferson arrived in Philadelphia in 1775 as a Virginia delegate to the Second Continental Congress, he was asked to write in favor of independence. When he returned the following year, he was appointed to a five-man committee, which included Benjamin Franklin and John Adams, to draft a formal declaration of independence from England. The Declaration of Independence was written almost entirely by Jefferson and was approved and signed by the other delegates to the congress on July 4, 1776.

THOMAS JEFFERSON
1743–1826

Jefferson was a member of the Virginia House of Delegates from 1776 to 1779. He introduced bills to reorganize the courts of law, to establish a system of public education, and to guarantee religious freedom in Virginia. He served two terms as governor of Virginia (1779–1781), then returned to his beloved Monticello, where he wrote his remarkable book, *Notes on Virginia*. In 1789, he became the first U.S. secretary of state under President George Washington.

In the presidential election of 1800, Aaron Burr and Thomas Jefferson received the same number of electoral votes. The election was decided by the House of Representatives in favor of Jefferson. Thus, he became the third president of the United States. In 1803, his minister to France bought the Louisiana Territory, nearly doubling the size of the United States.

Jefferson was easily reelected to the presidency in 1804. When his second term ended in 1809, he returned to Monticello and continued his campaign for a system of public education. His University of Virginia opened its doors in 1825.

When Jefferson died on July 4, 1826, he had written his own epitaph: "Author of the Declaration of Independence and of the Statute of Virginia for Religious Freedom, and Father of the University of Virginia." Although he had accomplished many things during his long life, these were the ones for which he most wanted to be remembered.

The ValueTale Series